Fish of the
Midwest

Adventure Quick Guides
YOUR WAY TO EASILY IDENTIFY FISH

Adventure Quick Guides

Organized by well-known fish groupings such as bass, pike and panfish, this guide covers 81 species of the most common sport fish found in the Midwest.

HOW TO USE THIS GUIDE

- Identify what fish group your catch belongs to and turn to that section. If you don't know, flip through the guide and compare your fish's general shape to that of the different groups. (Each fish grouping usually has a general shape in common.)

- Once you're in the right section, compare your fish to the illustrations. Key identifying features are listed for each species.

- The average weight and length for each sport fish are listed. Fish that are not commonly kept/weighed have no weights listed. If you want to know if you've caught a lunker, turn to the Records page in the back of the book. The record catches of the Midwest can be found there.

MIDWEST FISH FIELD GUIDES

For more information about each of these species, including details about habitat, similar species, range, diet and fascinating facts, check out Adventure's field guides for these Midwestern states: Illinois, Indiana, Michigan, Minnesota, Missouri, Ohio and Wisconsin.

ABOUT THE AUTHOR

Dave Bosanko is an avid fisherman and naturalist with a degree in Biology from the University of Minnesota. His work has included studies and field work in biodiversity. He has long enjoyed applying his extensive research to patterning fish location and behavior and observing how these fascinating species interact with one another in the underwater web of life.

IMAGE CREDITS

All images (with the exception of the Invasive Species page, see below) copyrighted by Timothy Knepp/USFWS, Duane Raver/USFWS and Joe Tomelleri. Cover image: Smallmouth Bass by David Hemenway.

Image credits for the Invasive Species page: Zebra Mussel courtesy of Amy Benson, USGS. Spiny Waterflea courtesy of Jeff Gunderson, Minnesota Sea Grant. Rusty Crayfish courtesy of USGS/Florida Biology. The following unaltered image on page 18 is licensed according to a Creative Commons 3.0 Attribution License, available here: http://creativecommons.org/licenses/by/3.0/us/. "Eurasian water-milfoil" by Alison Fox, University of Florida, Bugwood.org, image 1624031

Bass

Largemouth Bass
large forward-facing mouth; lower jaw extends to rear margin of eye

8–20"
1–5 lb.

Smallmouth Bass
red eyes; mouth does not extend beyond eye

6–20"
1–4 lb.

Spotted Bass
green sides with dark stripe; dark spots above the stripe; mouth does not extend beyond eye

6–18"
½–1 lb.

White Bass
silver sides with broken or indistinct stripes; lower jaw protrudes beyond snout

6–18"
½–2 lb.

Yellow Bass
silvery yellow to brassy sides; two sections of dorsal fin connected by membrane

8–12"
½–1 lb.

Striped Bass
bright silver sides; two sections of dorsal fin separated

18–30"
10–20 lb.

Panfish

Orangespotted Sunfish
blue-green back fading to lighter sides; black gill spot with light margin

3–4"
¼ lb.

Pumpkinseed
sides speckled with orange-yellow spots and striped with 7 to 10 vertical bands; gill spot with orange-red crescent on margin

6–8"
¼–½ lb.

Redear Sunfish
back and sides bronze to dark green with faint vertical bars; bluish stripes on side of head; gill flap short with dark spot and red margin in males

8–10"
½–1 lb.

Rock Bass
thick, heavy bronze body; each scale on sides has a dark spot; large mouth

8–10"
½–1 lb.

Warmouth
stout, lightly mottled body with faint vertical bands; large mouth; 3 to 5 reddish-brown streaks radiate from red eyes

11"
½–¾ lb.

Yellow Perch
sides have 6 to 9 olive-green vertical bars; front dorsal fin consists entirely of spines, back dorsal all soft rays

8–11"
⅜–⅝ lb.

Panfish

Black Crappie
silver sides with dark green to black blotches

7–12"
⅓–1 lb.

White Crappie
silvery green to white sides with 7 to 9 dark vertical bars

6–20"
1–4 lb.

Bluegill
5 to 9 dark vertical bars on sides; yellow belly and copper breast; large dark gill spot that extends completely to gill margin

6–9"
⅓–⅔ lb.

Flier
brown spots on sides; dark wedge-shaped bar under eye

4–6"
¼ lb.

Green Sunfish
dark olive to bluish sides with yellow-flecked scales; dark gill spot with pale margin

4–6"
¼–½ lb.

Longear Sunfish
light green sides flecked with blue or yellow; belly and chest bright orange to pale yellow; gill flap tapers into a long, black tab

3–4"
½ lb.

Pike

Muskellunge

dark vertical bars
or blotches on
silver-green
sides; dark
markings on
light background

30–40"
10–20 lb.

Northern Pike

light-green sides
with bean-shaped
light spots
on a dark
background;
head is long and
flattened in front

18–24"
2–5 lb.

Grass Pickerel

torpedo-shaped
olive green
body; wavy
yellowish
bars on sides

10–12"
½–1 lb.

Walleye

long, round, dark
silver or gold olive
body; white
spot on bottom
lobe of tail

6–18"
½–2 lb.

Sauger

slender gray, dark
silver or brown
body with dark
side blotches;
black spots on
spiny dorsal fin;
some white on lower
tail margin

10–12"
½–2 lb.

Brook Trout

worm-like markings
on back; lower
fins reddish
orange with white
leading edge

8–10"
½ lb.

Brown Trout

golden-brown to dark
olive back and
sides; spots on
sides, dorsal
fin and sometimes
upper lobe of tail

15–24"
1½–5 lb.

Lake Trout

gray-green head,
back, top fin and
tail; white spots
on sides and
unpaired fins;
deeply forked tail

15–20"
7–20 lb.

Rainbow Trout

blue-green to
brown head and
back; silver lower
sides with pink to
rose stripes; entire
body covered with
small black spots

10–12"
1 lb.

Salmon

Chinook Salmon

back is dark and silver below lateral line; small black spots on back and tail

8–20"
1–5 lb.

Coho Salmon

dark back with silver sides and belly; small dark spots on back, sides and upper half of tail

12–20"
4–5 lb.

Pink Salmon

blue-green back; sides turn pink during breeding season; dark spots on back and tail, some as big as its eye

17–19"
1–2 lb.

Cisco

body tinged pink or purple; lightly colored forked tail; jaws equal length or with a slight underbite

10–12"
1 lb.

Lake Whitefish

dark, forked tail; mouth small with two small flaps between openings of each nostril; snout protrudes past lower jaw

12–18"
3–5 lb.

Brown Bullhead

dark olive, yellowish-black
or mottled black
sides; rounded
tail; free adipose
fin; well-defined
barbs on pectoral fins

8–10"
¾–2 lb.

Blue Catfish

pale blue to dark bluish
gray back and sides;
forked tail; free
adipose fin

2–3'
20–30 lb.

Channel Catfish

silver-gray to dark
olive or slate back
and sides; forked
tail with pointed
lobes

10–20"
2–4 lb.

Flathead Catfish

color variable, usually
mottled yellow or
brown; belly
cream to yellow;
tail squared;
pronounced underbite

20–30"
10–20 lb.

White Catfish

bluish-silver body and
off-white belly;
forked tail with
rounded lobes;
white chin barbells

10–18"
1–2 lb.

Stonecats/Madtoms

dark olive to brown;
large, fleshy head;
madtoms have
a squared tail,
stonecats have a
rounded one

3–6"

Carp

Common Carp

brassy yellow to dark olive back and sides; round mouth has two pairs of barbels; reddish tail and anal fin; each scale has a dark margin

16–18"
5–20 lb.

Grass Carp

slender, compressed body with crosshatched appearance; large scales with a dark edge and black spot at base; upturned mouth with no barbels

18–30"
5–30 lb.

Goldfish

variable color, ranging from olive-green to orange, gold or pink; deep body; fins heavy and rounded

3–10"

Bighead Carp

dark gray to black back; silver-gray sides with dark blotches; low-set eyes; upturned mouth; tiny body scales; no scales on head

18–30"
5–40 lb.

Silver Carp

silver sides with a crosshatched pattern; upturned mouth; eyes far forward and low on head; tiny body scales; no scales on head

18–30"
5–40 lb.

Suckers

Bigmouth Buffalo
rounded back without a hump; long dorsal fin; large forward-facing mouth with thin lips

18–20"
10–12 lb.

Smallmouth Buffalo
deeply arched back with a pronounced hump; long dorsal fin; blunt snout; small downturned mouth

18–20"
10–20 lb.

Black Buffalo
slate-green to dark gray back and sides; slightly arched back; blunt nose; downturned mouth

15–20"
10–12 lb.

Quillback
bright silver back and sides, often with yellow tinge; fins clear; leading edge of dorsal fin extends into a large, arching "quill"

12–14"
1–2 lb.

Redhorse
blunt nose; downward pointed sucker mouth; lower fins and tail orange, red or rusty brown

8–12"
½–1 lb.

White Sucker
back olive-brown; sides gray-silver; dorsal and tail fins slate; lower fins tinged orange

12–18"
1–3 lb.

Hog Sucker
back dark olive-brown fading to yellow-brown blotches; 4 to 5 irregular dark saddles; lower fins are dull red

10–12"
1 lb.

Minnows

Fathead Minnow

dark sides; dark spot
on tail; rounded
snout and fins;
dark blotch on
dorsal fin

3–4"

Golden Shiner

sides golden; deep
slab-sided body;
mouth angled up;
long, triangular
head

3–7"

Redbelly Dace

sides with two broad bands
on tan background;
breeding males
have a bright red
belly, a female's is
yellow-orange

2–3"

Creek Chub

dark olive back;
silver-gray sides that
reflect purple; large
mouth; dark spot at
base of dorsal fin; small
barbel between upper
jaw and snout

2–3"

Mudminnow

tan to yellow-brown
sides with faint,
wavy vertical bars;
round tail; dark bar
just before tail

2–4"

Johnny Darter

sides tan to gold;
upper sides have
dark blotches;
lower sides have X, Y
or W patterns

2–4"

Minnows

Mosquitofish
scales have a crosshatched appearance; upturned mouth; dark bar under eye; rounded tail

2–3"

Stickleback
body narrows near tail; dorsal fin reduced to 4–5 separated spines; pelvic fin reduced to a single spine; sharp teeth

2–4"

Brook Silverside
sides silver-green with conspicuous light stripe; upturned mouth; two dorsal fins; deeply forked tail

3–4"

Blackstriped Topminnow
dark lateral stripe through lips to tail; spotted tail, dorsal and anal fins; upturned mouth

2–3"

Logperch
long cylindrical body with 15 to 25 dark vertical bands; conical snout overhanging mouth

3–6"

Primitive Fish

Bowfin

long, stout body; rounded
tail; continuous
dorsal fin;
bony plates
covering head; males
have a large "eye" spot at
the base of the tail

12–24"
2–5 lb.

Alligator Gar

rear fins and rear ¼ of body
spotted; body
encased in
hard, plate-like
scales; broad snout
shorter than rest of head;
two rows of large teeth on
each side of upper jaw

36–48"
30–40 lb.

Longnose Gar

dark spots along sides;
long body is
encased in hard,
plate-like scales; snout
twice as long as head

12–24"
2–5 lb.

Shortnose Gar

long body is encased
in hard,
plate-like scales;
snout ⅓ longer than head;
needle-sharp teeth

12–24"
1–3 lb.

Spotted Gar

spots on entire body, including
snout, fins
and tail;
cylindrical body; narrow
snout slightly longer than the
head; sharp teeth

12–18"
¾–2 lb.

Primitive Fish

Native Lampreys

eel-like body; round, sucking-disk mouth; seven paired gill openings; long, undivided dorsal fin extending to tail

6–12"

Sea Lamprey

eel-like body; round, sucking-disk mouth; seven paired gill openings; long and divided dorsal fin extending to tail

12–24"

Lake Sturgeon

tail is shark-like, with upper lobe longer than lower lobe; noticeable spiracles (gaps between the eye and corner of the gill)

36–60"
10–40 lb.

Shovelnose Sturgeon

tail shark-like, with upper lobe longer than lower lobe with a long filament; no spiracles; belly covered with scale plates

12–24"
2–3 lb.

Pallid Sturgeon

tail shark-like, with upper lobe longer than lower lobe with no filament; no spiracles; belly without scale plates

12–24"
2–3 lb.

Paddlefish

gray, scaleless body; snout protrudes into large paddle; gill extends into long, pointed flaps

24–48"
20–40 lb.

Goldeye

large yellow-tinged eyes; large scales; thin flattened body; leading edge of dorsal fin starts behind that of the anal fin

12–18"
1–2 lb.

Mooneye

large silver-tinged eyes; large scales; thin flattened body with a sharp scale ridge (keel) from throat to pelvic fin

12–18"
1–2 lb.

Freshwater Drum

gray back with purple or bronze reflections; silver sides; humped back; lateral line runs from head through the tail

10–18"
2–5 lb.

Sculpin

large wing-like pectoral fins; large mouth; eyes set almost on top of the head; scalloped anal fin

2–5"

Round Goby

scaled body; straight-edged anal fin; pelvic fin fused to form sucker-like disc

2–5"

Alewife

purple spot behind gill
and above pectoral fin;
large mouth
with protruding
lower jaw

4–8"

Skipjack Herring

large mouth with protruding
lower jaw; no dark spots
on shoulder;
blue-green
back that ends
abruptly on silver sides

12–16"
1–2 lb.

Gizzard Shad

snout protrudes over
small mouth; young fish
have a dark spot
on shoulder
behind the gill;
last rays of dorsal fin
form a long thread

6–8"
1–8 oz.

Threadfin Shad

lower jaw protrudes
beyond mouth;
yellow tail; last ray
of dorsal fin forms
a long thread

2–5"

Invasive Species

Eurasian Watermilfoil

Native to Europe/Asia and now spread by anglers, watermilfoil is found in many Midwestern water bodies, where it greatly disrupts the ecosystem

Spiny Waterflea

Microscopic animals that often clump together on fishing line and feed on important food sources for many native fish species

Zebra Mussel

Native to Asia, zebra mussels reproduce prolifically and cover lake bottoms, boats, docks and outcompete native species for food

Rusty Crayfish

Native to the eastern portion of the Midwest, they were used as bait and now threaten many waterways outside their range

How to Protect Our Midwestern Lakes and Rivers

Invasive species are hitchhikers, tagging along on boats, trailers, in bait buckets and on fishing gear. Everyone enjoying time on the water can help prevent invasive species from spreading with three easy steps: **Cleaning** all visible weeds and animals (mussels) from boats, trailers and fishing equipment; **Draining** equipment (livewell, motor, ballast, etc.); and **Drying** boats and equipment for five days after use. (Another option is to spray gear with a high-pressure washer/high-temperature water.) Also, dispose of bait legally by throwing it in the onshore trash. Dumping it in/near the lake is illegal. For more information, visit www.wildlifeforever.org/invasive-species

Records

SPECIES	RECORD	STATE CAUGHT
Largemouth Bass	14 pounds, 12 oz.	Indiana
Smallmouth Bass	11 pounds, 15 oz.	Kentucky
Striped Bass	64 pounds, 15 oz.	Nebraska
Muskellunge	69 pounds, 11 oz.	Wisconsin
Northern Pike	45 pounds, 12 oz.	Minnesota
Walleye	21 pounds, 8 oz.	Kentucky
White Crappie	4 pounds, 14 oz.	Kentucky
Bluegill	4 pounds, 3 oz.	Kentucky
Redear Sunfish	3 pounds, 10 oz.	Indiana
Brook Trout	12 pounds	South Dakota
Brown Trout	36 pounds, 11.5 oz.	Illinois
Lake Trout	61 pounds, 3 oz.	Michigan
Rainbow Trout	42 pounds, 8 oz.	Wisconsin
Chinook Salmon	46 pounds, 8 oz.	Michigan
Coho Salmon	30 pounds, 3 oz.	Michigan
Channel Catfish	55 pounds	South Dakota
Flathead Catfish	123 pounds	Kansas
Common Carp	67 pounds	Iowa

Fighting Ability

Some people fish to eat, whereas others enjoy the fight of reeling a fish in. This chart provides an unofficial ranking of how much of a fight you can expect from some of the more popular sport fish species. Perhaps surprisingly, the most popular fish (*e.g.* walleye) aren't always the best fighters.

Strong

Alligator Gar	Coho Salmon	Rainbow Trout
Bluegill	Common Carp	Smallmouth Bass
Bowfin Flathead	Lake Trout	Spotted Bass
Brown Trout	Largemouth Bass	Striped Bass
Buffalos	Longnose Gar	
Catfish	Muskellunge	
Chinook Salmon	Northern Pike	

Average

Brook Trout	Redear Sunfish	White Bass
Channel Catfish	Walleye	White Catfish

Poor

Brown Bullhead	White Crappie
Sauger	Yellow Perch

Table Quality

If you're fishing and looking to cook your catch, the following chart outlines some of the most popular game fish for the table. Of course, tastes are subjective, so the following list is too. Note: This list only covers the fish that are most commonly eaten.

Excellent

Black Crappie	Coho Salmon	Trout
Bluegill Brook	Lake Trout	Walleye
Brown Trout	Rainbow Trout	White Crappie
Channel Catfish	Sauger	Yellow Perch

Average

Brown Bullhead	Northern Pike	Striped Bass
Chinook Salmon	Redear Sunfish	White Bass
Flathead Catfish	Smallmouth Bass	White Catfish
Largemouth Bass	Spotted Bass	

Eaten by a Few

Bowfin	Common Carp
Buffalos	Muskellunge

Not Often Eaten

Alligator Gar	Longnose Gar

Adventure Quick Guides

Only Midwest Fish

Organized by common groups for quick and easy identification

Simple and convenient!
Narrow your choices by common group, and view just a few fish at a time.

- Pocket-sized format—easier than laminated foldouts

- Each species' average length and weight, as well as regional records

- Information about aquatic invasive species that threaten Midwestern lakes and waterways

- Based on Dave Bosanko's best-selling fish field guides

Improve your fish identification skills with the *Fish of the Midwest Playing Cards*

ISBN 978-1-59193-583-4   U.S. $9.95

SPORTS / FISHING / MIDWEST